PUTTING ON THE WHOLE ARMOR OF GOD

Alfred E. Adams

Ephesians 6:12 Publishing

Layout and Cover Design by Jacob Sparks
Editing by Susan B. Lunsford

God Built Alfred is an Evangelistic Association.

Missions Statement – is proclaiming the Gospel of the Lord Jesus
Christ to all we can by every effective means available to us and by
equipping the church and others to do the same.

PUTTING ON THE WHOLE ARMOR OF GOD
EPHESIANS 6:10-17

SPIRITUAL WARFARE

Lesson One

A Soldier in God's Army

Questions: How can I be a soldier for Christ? Am I a soldier in God's army? What type of soldier am I?

How can I be a better soldier for Christ?

A. Entering the Service of the Lord (verse 10) Many people limit Christianity to church membership, baptism, and attendance of religious services. Although these things will characterize the Christian life, Christianity is much more than this. Christianity is a personal relationship with Christ, which we enter through an act of our own will. This relationship has been made possible through the death, burial, and resurrection of Christ. By an act of my will, I place my faith in Christ alone for salvation. I willingly repent of my sins and turn from them to Christ as my only hope. As a result of being born again, I am in the family of God. He is my Father. I am His child. I am now in a spiritual family where other Christians are my brothers and sisters in Christ. I belong to a new family, the family of God! The body of Christ! I am no longer bound and blinded by Satan. I have been set free to serve Christ. I am no longer an enemy of God, but a child of the King and a soldier in His army. Yes, Christianity is a life of service, as a Christian soldier in God's army.

B. Example: How does a soldier get in the physical army? Enlist. What kind of soldier am I? Not all soldiers are the same. In the military, regular exams, physicals, and evaluation reports are used to track the progress of each soldier. In which of the following four categories am I?

1. **SPIES** they have the uniform of Christ and they talk a good talk. They are still enemies of God.
2. **AWOL** absent without leave! They joined but deserted.
3. **WOUNDED** they have been hurt by others or themselves and are not able to fight, need healing.
4. **TRAINED/READY** they are spiritually fit. They are willing and able to do any job which will benefit the cause of Christ.

C. Steps to Being a Better Soldier

1. "Be strong in the Lord, and the power of His might." This is not a physical battle and will not be won with physical strength. We need to be on a spiritual exercise program. We need to be active members of a local body of Christ.

2. "Put on the whole armor of God."-When you join the military you do not look, dress, or act like a civilian. When you join, you do not have to supply the equipment you need. We serve in the Lord's army, and He will supply all we need for victory.

3. "Stand firm" We need to have the highest level of commitment. Nothing in our lives should take priority over our spiritual service. Emotions or circumstances should have no effect on the completion of our mission. We are ready to follow the "King of kings" and our "Lord of lords" into any battle and fight to the death giving our very lives if need be, for the One who gave His life for us.

PUTTING ON THE WHOLE ARMOR OF GOD
EPHESIANS 6:10-17

SPIRITUAL WARFARE

Lesson Two

Understanding our Enemy

A. Satan's Past. Satan was not always like he is today. Satan was once an anointed cherub or angel. Satan's original home was in heaven serving and worshipping Almighty God. Ezekiel 28:14 teaches that as an angel Satan was an "anointed cherub," "perfect in beauty," "full of wisdom," "upon the holy mountain of God," "wasn't perfect in thy ways." His angelic name was Lucifer meaning "the son of the morning," "the shining one," or "the day star." Ezekiel 28 also reveals that Lucifer lifted up his heart with pride which led to self-exaltation and rebellion against God. Isaiah 14:12-15 gives a detailed description of Lucifer's sin which led to his expulsion from heaven. This great fallen angel (Lucifer) is the one we know as Satan. Since this early time in eternity past, Satan has been the enemy of God. His entire being and purpose is to wage spiritual war against God and His most cherished creation, mankind.

B. Satan's Personality. Satan is the most bitter enemy of God and His people. Scripture reveals Satan's personality through the names which identify him. "tempter" Matthew 4:3. "murderer" John 8:44. "liar" John 8:44. "evil one" I John 5:19. "deceiver" Revelation 12:9. "accuser of the brethren" Revelation 12:10. Seeking to hide his true personality, Satan portrays himself as an angel of light.   2 Corinthians 11:14.

C. Satan's Position. Ephesians 6:12. Scripture gives three titles for Satan which reveal his position.

1. Prince "the prince of this world" John 12:31"the prince of the power of the air" Ephesians 2:2-Scripture is clear that Satan is the head of evil men and evil spirits.

2.Ruler "rulers of the darkness of this world" Ephesians 6:12 Satan is ruler or leader of evil men and evil spirits.

3. god "god of this age" 2 Corinthians 4:4 Satan's original desire was to set himself up above God and be like God. As an imposter, he has set himself up as the god of this world. New Testament scripture reveals this in several ways. a. Reference to synagogue of Satan –Revelation 2:9b. Ministers of Satan –2 Corinthians 11c. Gospel of Satan – Galatians 1d. Satan has his own communion table and cup -1 Corinthians 10:20-21

D. Satan's Power Ephesians 6:12 According to scripture, Satan is the second most powerful person in the universe. The power of God Himself is the only power which can conquer and destroy Satan. Scripture reveals Satan has real power. 1.Power to destroy 2. Power to bind and bound 3.Power of darkness 4.Power of the air 5.Power of death-Satan is described as both a roaring lion and a great dragon.-Satan has his own armor, spiritual army, strongholds, weapons and is a very powerful enemy. Every person who has ignored or underestimated this enemy has paid with their lives and eternal souls.

E. Satan's Purpose Ephesians 6:11-12 John 10:10 is a vivid statement revealing the heart of Satan's purpose. "The thief cometh not, but for to kill, and to steal and to destroy:" John

10:10a-Three major purpose are revealed:1. Steal –Satan wants to steal the very throne of God. He wants to steal the hearts of God's creation. Our enemy wants to steal the joy of our salvation. 2. Kill –Satan who did not hesitate to seek to murder Christ, has every intention of killing every human he can. He wants us to die physically and he wants us to spend eternity in spiritual death. 3. Destroy –Satan wants to destroy God and God's children. Satan wants to destroy marriage and the family which God instituted. Satan wants to destroy the church of Jesus Christ. -The word "wiles" in verse 11 means strategy or plans. (war plans) -Satan has a detailed plan to accomplish his purpose. -We are told five times in Ephesians 6:11-12 to "stand against" Satan and the fulfillment of his purpose.

PUTTING ON THE WHOLE ARMOR OF GOD
EPHESIANS 6:10-17
SPIRITUAL WARFARE

Lesson Three

Our Armor of Defense (Part 1)

Twice in Ephesians 6:10-17, we are told to "put on the whole armor of God."1. In verse 11 we are told to put it on so we might "stand against the wiles of the devil." 2. In verse 13 we are urged to put on the armor so "that you may be able to with stand in the evil day, and having done all, to stand." In verses 14-17, we find five pieces of armor that are given for our defense. 1. Belt of truth (v. 14) 2. Breastplate of righteous (v. 14) 3. Shoes of the gospel of peace (v. 15) 4. Shield of faith (v. 16) 5. Helmet of salvation (v. 17) For study purposes, we will look at these pieces of armor individually. However, this is a single suit of armor and should be put on in its entirety. Christ has supplied all we need to be victorious in spiritual battle, but it is each believer's responsibility to use what the Lord has provided.

Our Armor of Defense

I. Girdle (belt) of truth (v. 14) A. Physical applications of the belt-This belt was commonly worn by Romans and was always worn by soldiers. The belt was usually 4 to 6 inches wide and fastened around the middle. The belt was made of leather or linen. -Many times the belt would support an apron that hung down, covering the soldier's groin.-The belt was worn outside the flowing robe that was commonly worn in Paul's day.-We have all read the statement in scripture to "gird up your loins." This is getting in the position for battle.

-In preparation for battle the soldiers would pull up the robe and tuck it under the belt.

Spiritual applications of the belt This is the belt of "TRUTH"-What is truth? John 17:17 says "thy word is truth." In John 14:16 Jesus said, "I am the way, the TRUTH, and the life." To put on the TRUTH is literally to put on the word of God and Christ. Steps to putting on the belt of TRUTH. 1. We need to KNOW the truth (2 Timothy 2:15) 2. We need to BELIEVE the truth (1 Thessalonians 2:13) 3. We need to ACT on the truth (James 1:22-25) Satan is the father of lies, but he can never stand against the truth.

II. Breastplate of Righteousness Two types of breastplates were worn by Roman soldiers.1. One was made by joining several broad, curved metal bands together using leather laces. 2. The second was a type of chain mail, constructed by joining many small metal rings together to form a vest. The purpose of the breastplate was to form a barrier of defense for the soldier's vital organs. A. The Position of Righteousness When we receive Christ as our Savior by faith, we enter into a position of righteousness before God. Philippians 3:9 says, "And be found in him, not having mine own righteousness, which is of the law, but that which is through the faith of Christ, the righteousness which is of God by faith." II Corinthians 5:21 says, "For he hath made him to be sin for us, who knew no sin; that we might be made the righteousness of God in him." This is a symbol that Christ himself is protecting us in this spiritual battle.

B. The Practice of Righteousness Most Christians accept their position of righteousness but do little to practice righteousness. We need to become in practice, what we have been made in position. Our positional righteousness will win the war, but our practical righteousness will cause us to win or lose daily spiritual battles. Ephesians 4:24 says "that you put on the new man which was created according to God, in true righteousness and holiness." If we fail to live out our righteousness, we become easy targets for our enemy.

C. The Protection of Righteousness The main purpose of the breastplate was to protect the heart. The heart is the most vital organ. In the spiritual battle the heart is also especially important, because it is the seat of our emotions. Whoever wins the battle for the heart, will win the spiritual battle. As we live out our position of righteousness in Christ, through living righteously, our hearts fall more and more in love with Christ. If Christ rules our hearts, then he rules our emotions, and we will prove strong warriors in the spiritual battle.

PUTTINGON THE WHOLE ARMOR OF GOD
EPHESIANS 6:10-17

SPIRITUAL WARFARE

Lesson Four Our Armor of Defense (Part 2)

III. Shoes of the Gospel of Peace (v.15) A. Practical Application of the Shoes The Roman soldier's shoes were made of thick leather, with straps that tied to the soldier's lower leg.-Sometimes the soles were made of wood and covered with leather for comfort. Many times, the shoes would be studded with nails on the bottom for better traction. Soldiers marching into battle needed a firm foundation. The word translated "prepared" or "readiness" in verse 15 can also be translated a "firm foundation." The soldier marched into battle with his shoes, and the shoes provided a firm foundation when the battle was raging.

B. Spiritual Application of the Shoes of the Gospel of Peace The Christian needs a special kind of shoes for the spiritual battle (shoes of the gospel of peace.) The "gospel" is the fact that God has sent His only Son, Jesus into the world. Christ has lived a sinless life in the flesh. Jesus Christ has died on the cross for our sins and shed His blood for our cleansing. He arose victorious on the third day over death, hell, and the grave. He is coming again!! The "peace" is the adoption of this gospel and Christ into my life by faith. The "gospel of peace" affects the spiritual battle in three areas: 1. Peace with God (Salvation) 2. Peace with other Christians (Unity) 3. Peace with circumstance (Absence of worry)

C. How to Put on the "Shoes of the Gospel of Peace" 1. We need a personal relationship with the author of peace.

"For God is not the author of confusion, but of peace..." (1 Corinthians 14:33) 2. We need to keep our attention on the Prince of Peace. "You will keep him in perfect peace, whose mind is stayed on you." (Isaiah 26:3) 3. We need to allow the Spirit of God to control our lives. "The fruit of the Spirit is love, joy, peace..." (Galatians 5:22) 4. We need to pray about everything. "Don't worry about anything, but pray about everything, and the peace of God will guard your hearts and minds..." (Phil. 4:6) 5. We need to love God's Word. "Great peace have those who love your law." (Psalm 119:165) Jesus has given us His peace for the spiritual battle, but we must put it on. (John 14:27)

IV. The Shield of Faith (v. 16) A. Practical Application of the Shield (v. 16)-The Roman soldier's shield was made of wood, and then covered with animal skin.-A typical shield for the Roman period would be four feet long and three feet wide.-Many times iron was molded around the edges to strengthen the shield. -A leather strap or wooden handle was attached to the back, by which the soldier could hold and maneuver the shield during battle.-Many times the soldiers would form a barrier by putting their shields side by side.-Roman soldiers would soak their shields in water, so flaming arrows would not burn up the shield-The shield would protect the soldier from exposed areas of weakness in the armor.

B. Spiritual Application of the "Shield of Faith" Our spiritual shield is not wood or metal but "FAITH!" Galatians 2:20 says "I have been crucified with Christ; it is no longer I who live, but Christ lives in me; and the life which I now live in the flesh I live by FAITH in the Son of God, who loved me and gave Himself for me." We see yet again; this is another way of saying we need to put on Jesus Christ and allow Him to be our defense." We need to answer three main questions: 1. What is faith? Hebrews 11:1 answers that question. "Now faith is the substance of things hoped for, the evidence of things not seen." Faith is not a doctrine, theology, fairy tale, myth or wonderful working of my imagination. Faith is "substance" and "evidence" 2. Where does faith come from? Romans 10:17 says, "So then faith cometh by hearing, and hearing by the word of God." Faith is something concrete, produced only by God's Holy Word. 3. How do I "take up" the shield of faith? We "take up" our faith by fixing our eyes on Jesus. Problems, temptations, circumstances, tragedy, fear, doubt, death, and every imaginable evil will rage around us during this spiritual battle. Hebrews 12:2 says, "Looking unto Jesus the author and finisher of our faith...." As we unwaveringly fix our eyes on Jesus, the Shield of His Faith rises between us and our enemy, (Satan) to shield us from every flaming arrow of the one who would wound and kill us.

PUTTING ON THE WHOLE ARMOR OF GOD
EPHESIANS 6:10-17

SPIRITUAL WARFARE

Lesson Five Our Armor of Defense (Part 3)

V. The Helmet of Salvation (v.17) A. Practical Application of the Helmet During the Roman period, the soldier's helmet was made from bronze or iron. To make the helmet more comfortable, the soldier would cover his head or line his helmet with cloth. The helmets would have a large strip of dyed horsehair down the top center. The different colors of this hair distinguished rank. The helmet usually covered part of the face and the back of the neck. The helmet provided protection from head injuries in hand-to-hand combat and falling debris.

C. Spiritual Application of the Helmet Our spiritual helmets are "salvation." Before I can put something on, I must understand what it is that I am putting on, or I may put on the wrong thing. 1. Correct Identification of "Salvation" Many people have tried to put on "salvation" by putting on religion, good works, church membership, baptism, biblical knowledge, suffering, poverty, legalism, false gods, and an endless host of other powerless imitations. If these things are not salvation, then what is salvation? The Bible records in Luke 2:30 that Simeon said, "For mine eyes have seen thy salvation." Salvation is a person! The person is Jesus Christ! Acts 4:12 says, "Neither is there salvation in any other: for there is none other name under heaven given among men, whereby we must be saved." To put on the helmet of salvation is literally to put on Jesus Christ. 2. How to put on "Salvation"-Jesus said in Luke 13:3,5 "Except ye repent, ye shall all likewise perish." Repent means to change your mind. It is a change of mind that leads to a change of action and direction. Romans 10:9-10 says, "That if you confess with your mouth, 'Jesus is Lord,' and believe in your heart that God raised Him from the dead, you will be saved. For itis with your heart that you believe and are justified, and it is with your mouth that you confess and are saved." We must make a personal profession of Christ as our Savior.

We must place a personal faith in Christ and Christ alone as our Savior

D. How the Helmet of Salvation Helps in Spiritual Battle 1. It is a sign of His "Lordship" in my life. Romans 14:8 says, "For whether we live, we live unto the Lord; and whether we die, we die unto the Lord: whether we live therefore, or die, we are the Lord's." 2. It means Christ's victory has become my victory. I Corinthians 15:57 says, "But thanks be to God, which giveth us the victory through our Lord Jesus Christ." 3. It allows us to win the battle of the "mind." I Corinthians 2:16 says, "But we have the mind of Christ." I Peter 1:13a says, "Wherefore gird up the loins of your mind..."

Once you have put on the Armor of God, please be mindful no where in the Bible it tells us to take it off. Also, do self-maintenance check your Armor for cracks. Cracks are low times in your life, the devil might not be able to defeat you with your Armor on, but he will try to wear you out. When times like this happens, take a break from the world and fast for a day, renew your mind, and then get back into the fight.

A call to Salvation.

"Dear Lord Jesus,

I am sorry for all the things I have done wrong: for the way I have turned my back on You, for the people I have hurt, for the people I have cheated. Lord, I ask You to come into my heart TODAY. Take my life and make it clean on the inside. I ask You to be my Lord and Savior. Help me now to live for You, to the glory of God. Amen.

May the Lord Bless you and Keep you

www.ingramcontent.com/pod-product-compliance
Lightning Source LLC
Chambersburg PA
CBHW060609030426
42337CB00019B/3682